Maps and Globes

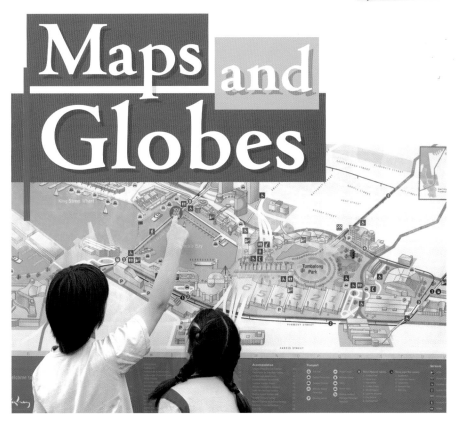

Written by Rebecca Olien

Table of Contents

Introduction

Have you ever heard the expression "You can't get there from here"?

Well, you can get there from here if you have a map. A map can help you see how you can travel to any place in the world.

In this book, you'll find out about maps and globes and how to use them.

A **map** is a flat drawing that shows where a place is, or the **location** of a place. A map can show you the entire world, but it can also show you a much smaller area, such as a state, or even a city park. What kinds of maps have you used?

Every map includes special features that help you read the map. Look at the map of the United States, and name the features. How does each feature help you understand the map?

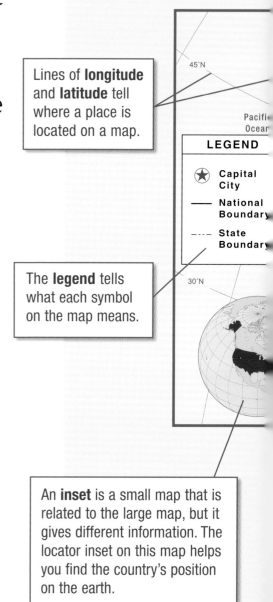

Lines of **longitude** and **latitude** tell where a place is located on a map.

45°N

Pacific Ocean

LEGEND

★ Capital City

—— National Boundary

---- State Boundary

The **legend** tells what each symbol on the map means.

30°N

An **inset** is a small map that is related to the large map, but it gives different information. The locator inset on this map helps you find the country's position on the earth.

The United States of America

120°W 105°W 90°W 75°W 60°W

45°N

Atlantic Ocean

Washington, D.C. ★

30°N

N
W   E
S

Alaska

Hawaii

0 100 Miles   500 Miles

0   500 KM

The **scale** shows how much smaller the map is than the real area it represents. Use it to figure out the distance between places.

The **compass rose** is a design on a map that shows direction. The tips on this one point to north (N), south (S), east (E), and west (W).

A **globe** is a model of Earth that shows you the sizes and shapes of land and water forms. Distances from one place to another are shown more accurately on a globe than on a flat map. So, why would you use a flat map if globes are more accurate?

Flat maps can be used for many more things, such as finding and comparing information about specific places. They're also easier to use. You can't fold up a globe and carry it in your backpack. Which would you use more often—a map or a globe?

A flat map is easy to use, but folding it can be tricky!

On the flat map, it's hard to see how close Alaska and Russia are to one another—the globe gives a more realistic picture.

Alaska

Russia

Atlantic
Ocean

Russia

Arctic
Ocean

Alaska

Indian
Ocean

Atlantic
Ocean

Latitude and Longitude

Many maps and globes have lines on them that form a grid over the earth. These imaginary lines—called lines of **latitude** and **longitude**—can help you find the exact location of any place in the world.

Lines of latitude run across the map or globe. They are measured in degrees (°) north and degrees south. Lines of longitude run up and down. They are measured in degrees east and degrees west.

Hundreds of years ago, explorers used these lines to help them find new lands. Today, people still use these lines to find their way.

At 0° latitude, the equator has some of the earth's warmest temperatures. Temperatures get colder as you move north and south away from the equator.

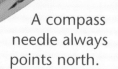

A compass needle always points north.

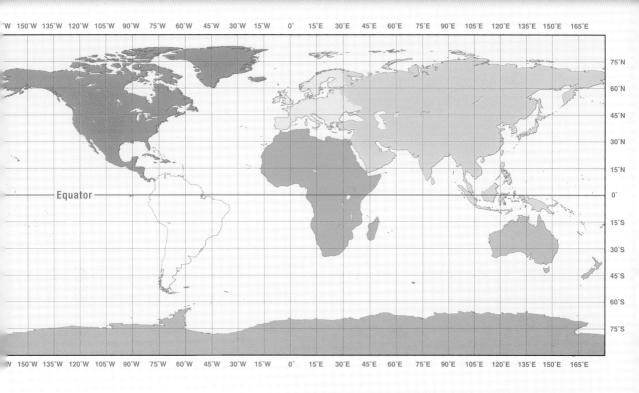

Equator

75°N
60°N
45°N
30°N
15°N
0°
15°S
30°S
45°S
60°S
75°S

Many ancient maps were inaccurate, like the shape of North America on the left side of this map.

Cartographers

A cartographer makes maps. In ancient times, mapmakers had to use their own observations or word of mouth to make maps. Today, cartographers use computers and land, aerial, and satellite photographs.

Here's how to use longitude and latitude. On the map below, place a finger on 45° N latitude and 105° E longitude. Move your fingers over the lines until they meet. What country are you in? Now use the map to play "Name That Country" on the next page.

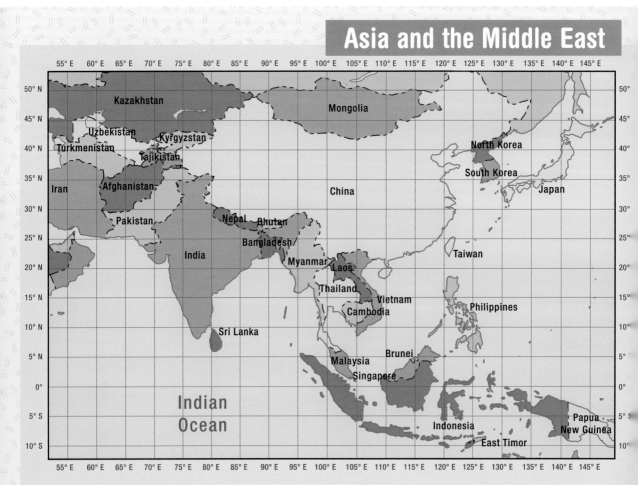

Asia and the Middle East

Name That Country

Use the lines of latitude and longitude on the map to name the country where you'll find each place shown below.

The Taj Mahal is located in this country at 20° N latitude and 80° E longitude.

The floating markets are located in this country at 15° N latitude and 100° E longitude.

The Great Wall is located in this country at 30° N latitude and 115° E longitude.

Mt. Everest is located in this country at 28° N latitude and 83° E longitude.

Different Kinds of Maps

A well-done map is like a snapshot—it gives you a lot of information in a glance. Just by looking at a map, you can learn many things about a place, from its climate to what land is best for growing crops.

Climate

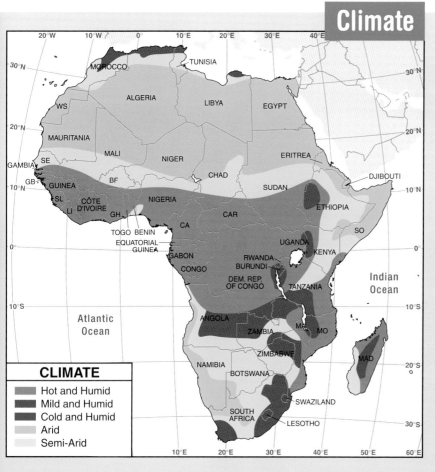

CLIMATE

- Hot and Humid
- Mild and Humid
- Cold and Humid
- Arid
- Semi-Arid

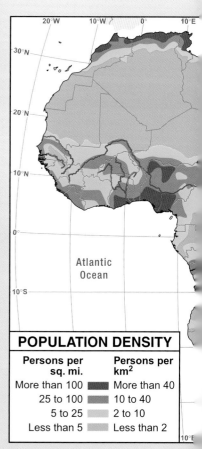

POPULATION DENSITY

Persons per sq. mi.	Persons per km²
More than 100	More than 40
25 to 100	10 to 40
5 to 25	2 to 10
Less than 5	Less than 2

Look at the three basic maps of Africa. Notice how each one gives you different information by using colors and shapes. Based on these three maps, how would you describe the northern part of Africa?

Population Density

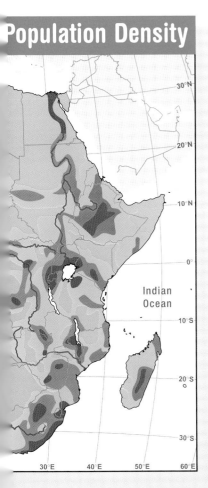

Agriculture

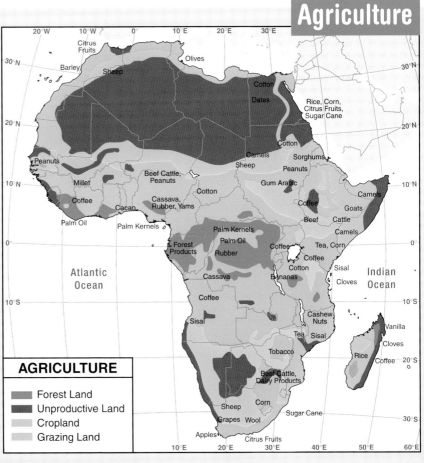

AGRICULTURE

- Forest Land
- Unproductive Land
- Cropland
- Grazing Land

ISLANDIA.

A radar map helps Californians prepare for a storm before it even arrives.

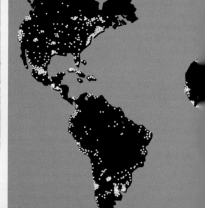

14

Hundreds of years ago, maps were drawn by hand. Many of them were covered with pictures that made them look like works of art. Though these maps may look strange to us, some of them were very accurate.

Today cartographers use modern instruments and techniques to create very precise maps. With these tools, they can map an approaching storm, the world's growing population, or even a busy harbor in the ocean.

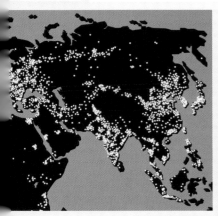

A world population map shows where people live.

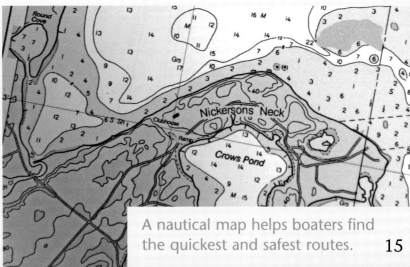

A nautical map helps boaters find the quickest and safest routes.

Now that you know how to read and
understand maps, you can get from here to
there. Think about all of the different places
where you see maps and how you use them.